Instructor's Guide

for

Creating Your High School Portfolio

and

Creating Your High School Resume

Second Edition

Christina C. Brunette,
Kathryn Kraemer Troutman,
and
JIST Editors

Instructor's Guide for *Creating Your High School Portfolio* and *Creating Your High School Resume*, Second Edition

© 2003 by JIST Publishing, Inc.

Published by JIST Works, an imprint of JIST Publishing, Inc.
8902 Otis Avenue
Indianapolis, IN 46216-1033

Phone: 800-648-JIST   Fax: 800-JIST-FAX
E-mail: info@jist.com   Web site: www.jist.com

Note to instructors. This instructor's guide is part of a curriculum that includes a portfolio workbook (*Creating Your High School Portfolio*, Second Edition) and a resume-writing workbook (*Creating Your High School Resume*, Second Edition). This guide covers both workbooks. The workbooks can be used separately or together, depending on your class objectives. This instructor's guide will be useful to you when it is used with one or both of the workbooks. All materials are available separately from JIST.

Videos on portfolio development, resumes, and job search topics are also available from JIST. A CD-ROM and Web site with information on over 14,000 jobs is available through CareerOINK.com. The Web site offers information at free and subscription levels. Call 1-800-648-JIST for details.

Quantity discounts are available for JIST products. Please call 1-800-648-JIST or visit www.jist.com for a free catalog and more information.

Visit www.jist.com. Find out about our products, order a catalog, and link to other career-related sites. You can also learn more about JIST authors and JIST training available to professionals.

Acquisitions Editor: Susan Pines
Development Editor: Veda Dickerson
Copy Editor: Stephanie Koutek
Cover and Interior Designer: Aleata Howard
Page Layout Coordinator: Carolyn J. Newland
Proofreader: Jeanne Clark

Printed in the United States of America

07 06 05 04 03   9 8 7 6 5 4 3 2 1

We have been careful to provide accurate information throughout this book, but it is possible that errors and omissions have been introduced. Please consider this in making any career plans or other important decisions. Trust your own judgment above all else and in all things.

Trademarks: All brand names and product names used in this book are trade names, service marks, trademarks, or registered trademarks of their respective owners.

ISBN 1-56370-908-2

About This Instructor's Guide

Instructor's Guide for Creating Your High School Portfolio and Creating Your High School Resume, Second Edition, was created to accompany two separate student workbooks that are published by JIST Works:

> *Creating Your High School Portfolio: An Interactive Guide for Documenting and Planning Your Education, Career, and Life,* Second Edition

> *Creating Your High School Resume: A Step-by-Step Guide to Preparing an Effective Resume for Jobs, College, and Training Programs,* Second Edition

While both workbooks are clear and self-explanatory, this instructor's guide will help you emphasize important points and lead students through the material as desired. This instructor's guide consists of three parts:

- **Part I** features unique career exploration and planning activities that are designed to help you integrate the two workbooks. This part was conceived and written by Christina C. Brunette, a teacher with over 30 years of classroom experience. She has been involved with school district advisory committees and has been recognized with several teaching honors.

- **Part II** contains teaching hints and transparency masters for *Creating Your High School Portfolio,* Second Edition. This part was compiled by JIST editors, based on material in the portfolio workbook.

- **Part III** provides you with teaching hints and transparency masters for *Creating Your High School Resume,* Second Edition. Resume expert Kathryn Kraemer Troutman wrote Part III. She is the author of *Creating Your High School Resume,* Second Edition, and two other resume books. She is the owner of The Resume Place and has written thousands of resumes for students and professionals.

Table of Contents

PART I

Career Exploration and Planning Activities

Featuring material to use with either or both
Creating Your High School Portfolio and
Creating Your High School Resume

By Christina C. Brunette

Overview

Part I contains activities that serve as a user-friendly guide for high school teachers and counselors who assist their students in creating portfolios and resumes. Lesson activities are based on material in the two companion texts:

Creating Your High School Portfolio: An Interactive Guide for Documenting and Planning Your Education, Career, and Life

Creating Your High School Resume: A Step-by-Step Guide to Preparing an Effective Resume for Jobs, College, and Training Programs

Although each text can stand alone, this part provides you with a practical, organized format that combines two interrelated topics—portfolios and resumes. Lessons in this part correlate to selected worksheets in both books. Additional activities are suggested for curricular extension and enrichment.

Today's instructor is frequently asked to add more content to the curricular plate, frustrating even the most conscientious individual. This part allows you to integrate instruction related to portfolio and resume work, saving time and effort. With your inspiration and this section's simple design and format, you can provide thought-provoking activities for high school students who are planning ahead for jobs and careers.

These activities, used in conjunction with the two companion texts, will enable high school students to do the following:

- Look at themselves as valuable people.
- Consider what they can do as future job holders.
- Explore their job options.
- Create resumes and portfolios.
- Make success happen for themselves.

Everyone in the workplace will benefit from the rippling effects these experiences can afford.

Before You Begin

The activities described in this part follow a considered order. Your students will begin by looking at their interests, values, and strengths. Next, they will examine their skills and explore the job opportunities available in the community. They will identify their own networks and, using relevant information, check the current job markets. Throughout the activities presented in this part, your students will compile data to include in their portfolios and resumes.

© JIST Works

Format of the Activities in Part I

Each activity is listed by the following:

- Activity number
- Activity name
- Curricular objective
- Format (for example, group, pairs, or individual)
- Resources (for example, text pages, paper and pencil, computer access and disk)

In addition, you will be able to cross-reference each activity with its companion text(s) by the page numbers included in the activity.

Useful Tips

1. All activities relate, directly or through extension, to one or both of the companion texts (*Creating Your High School Portfolio* and *Creating Your High School Resume*).

2. Follow the activities in order from Activity 1 to Activity 2, and so on. The contents of the two texts are woven into a usable, practical chronology in this section. If you follow this recommendation, you will *not* be going through the two companion texts page by page.

3. If you prefer to use each text sequentially, please see the tables on pages 52–54. There you will find *Creating Your High School Portfolio* and *Creating Your High School Resume* pages listed in sequence and cross-referenced with the Part I activity numbers.

4. The activities in this part give you guidance and extended suggestions for use with posted companion text pages.

5. Questions in italics are possible queries for your students. Other text is written primarily for your consideration.

Oftentimes, teachers and counselors have agendas so full that additional work seems impossible. This part's integration of *Creating Your High School Portfolio* and *Creating Your High School Resume* will enable you to guide your students through important, decision-making experiences aimed at preparing them for future employment and satisfying careers.

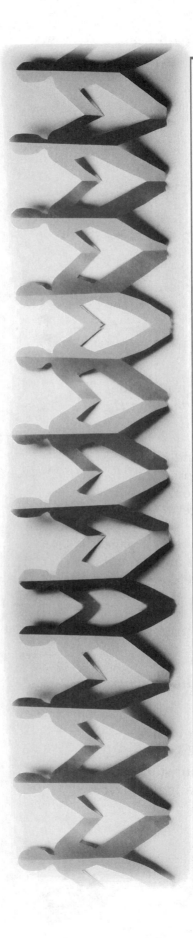

WHO ARE YOU?

Overall Objective

The student will develop individual decision-making and communications skills applicable to choosing a job.

COMPANION TEXT REFERENCE PAGES

Creating Your High School Portfolio:
Pages 7–11, 14–15, 33–36, and 38–53

Activity 1

Personal Value Comparisons

Objective: Students will examine their personal values and compare them to the values of their classmates.

Format: Group discussion, pairs work.

Resources: *Creating Your High School Portfolio*—pages 14–15 and 33–35, paper and pencil.

Ask students to read "Values" on pages 14–15. Allow time for them to complete "One Important Thing" on page 15. Ask students to name some of their values. Generate a class list of up to 10 widely accepted values. Next, ask students to scan the lists on pages 33–35 and to read the first two paragraphs under "Values" on page 33. Direct them to do the activities on pages 34–35. After they have finished, pair students together and let them share their lists with their partners. Finally, discuss as a group the similarities and differences of individual values versus the class list generated earlier. *How can personal values influence a person's career or job choices?* ■

Activity 2

Learning Styles

Objective: Students will explore their learning styles.

Format: Individual work, group discussion.

Resources: *Creating Your High School Portfolio*—pages 9–11 and 35–36, learning style survey, school counselor, psychology or sociology instructor, paper and pencil.

Ask students to read pages 9–11. Discuss the nine learning categories. Arrange for your school's counselor or psychology/sociology teacher to administer a learning style survey. Results should remain confidential unless students choose to share them. Ask students to read pages 35–36 and complete "My Learning Style." Discuss how students' learning styles will affect their career and job success. ■

Activity 3

Job Talks

Objective:	A representative group of students will plan and organize a job talk series.
Format:	Committee work.
Resources:	*Creating Your High School Portfolio*—pages 38–48, parents, colleagues, local community workers, calendar.

Assign a committee to plan a series of job talks throughout this course. Direct the group to compose a list of key questions for each guest. Questions should include the expected "What do you do in your job?" and "What job qualifications are required?" Students should also focus on those questions that involve problem solving, communications, and interpersonal skills. See pages 38–48 in *Creating Your High School Portfolio*. Identify guest job holders (parents, colleagues, local community workers, and so on) and then ask the committee to contact workers and set up sharing dates. Send the key questions to each guest speaker prior to class visits. ■

Activity 4

Job Seminars

Objective:	Students will plan a job seminar.
Format:	Seminar.
Resources:	Community workers, paper and pencil.

An option: If time constraints prevent a series of job talks, hold a job seminar with a panel of parent and community workers. Let your students prepare questions for these guests. Be sure to have students write thank-you notes to anyone who shares information with your class. ■

© JIST Works

Activity 5

Workplace Priorities

Objective:	Students will consider priorities of people in selected workplaces.
Format:	Group discussion, individual work.
Resources:	*Creating Your High School Portfolio*—page 42, paper and pencil.

Ask your students if they ever run out of time and why they think that happens! Discuss the concept of "priorities" as it relates to the country, to a teacher, to a doctor, to a fast-food server, and so on. Ask for volunteers to state a high priority in their own lives. Direct students to read "Managing Time" on page 42. Next allow a few minutes for students to jot down at least three high and three low priorities in their lives. Ask students to chart the minutes or blocks of time they commit to their high and low priorities during the next week. Instruct them to compare the times given to both sets of priorities and to analyze their findings. ■

Activity 6

Taking Good Care of Yourself

Objective:	Students will organize a seminar on "Taking Good Care of Yourself."
Format:	Seminar, individual work.
Resources:	*Creating Your High School Portfolio*—pages 43–48, principal, custodian, guidance counselor, cafeteria worker, paper and pencil.

Ask students to read pages 43–48. Hold a seminar about taking good care of yourself physically and emotionally. Invite a variety of participants, including the principal, a custodian, a guidance counselor, and a cafeteria worker. Require students to take notes during the seminar and to write a reflection about this experience. Ask students to consider whether they take good care of themselves and how their overall health affects their jobs as students. ■

Activity 7

Life Roles and Personal Priorities

Objective:	Students will consider all their life roles and relate them to their priorities and values.
Format:	Individual work, group discussion.
Resources:	*Creating Your High School Portfolio*—pages 48–49, paper and pencil.

Ask your students to make a mental list of all the "hats" they wear each day, week, and month. Discuss as a group some of their life roles. Direct them to recall their priorities and values. Allow a few minutes for students to fill out "My Changing Life Roles" on page 49. *Do the hats, or roles, blend sensibly with the priorities and values? If not, why not?* ■

Activity 8

Factors That Shape Life Roles

Objective:	Students will examine, compare, and contrast factors that shape our life roles.
Format:	Individual work, roundtable discussion.
Resources:	*Creating Your High School Portfolio*—pages 50–51, table, paper and pencil.

Let students have a few minutes to read pages 50–51 and then pick a couple of important factors that shape our life roles, such as gender, culture, and ethnicity. Hold a roundtable discussion regarding these issues. Divide the class into smaller groups, each group discussing one of the three issues. Compare and contrast the influences as your students see them. Let students complete the "My Roles and Decisions" on page 51. ■

Activity 9

Time Spent in Life Roles

Objective: Students will tally the time they spend in their life roles.

Format: Individual work for two-week assignment.

Resources: Two-week calendar, paper and pencil or computer spreadsheet and disk.

Assign your students a tracking job. For a two-week period, ask students to keep an hourly log of the various roles they assume throughout this time. Students should tally their minutes, by role, when time is up. Are there any surprises? Ask students to write a brief reflection piece about the outcome. ■

Activity 10

Life Dreams, Roles, Changes, and Goals

Objective: Students will consider their life dreams, life roles, life changes, and goals.

Format: Pairs work and small-group work.

Resources: *Creating Your High School Portfolio*—pages 7–9 and 50, clock for time checks.

Establish pairs for discussion. Allowing a total of 15–20 minutes, including directions, ask students to complete "Balancing My Life Roles" on page 50. Each student takes a one-minute turn for the first question, then the second question, and so on. Each person gets an opportunity to speak uninterrupted during his or her turn. Ask students to read pages 7–9 and to discuss how their life goals affect their dreams, roles, and changes. Ask how their dreams, roles, and changes affect the students' portfolios. ■

Activity 11

Priorities and Analysis of Career Interests

Objective: Students will prioritize and analyze their career
              interests.

Format: Individual work.

Resources: *Creating Your High School Portfolio*—pages
              33–34 and 52–53, paper and pencil.

Direct students to prioritize their career interests as listed on pages 52–53.
Next, ask them to read pages 33–34 and to analyze their top three career
interests in relationship to the job criteria listed on page 34. They should
complete this task in writing so it can be included in their portfolios. ■

WHAT CAN YOU DO?

Overall Objective

The student will systematically explore his or her skills and begin to collect data that will be used in formulating a portfolio and resume.

COMPANION TEXTS REFERENCE PAGES

Creating Your High School Portfolio:
Pages 3–6, 13, 16, 27–30, 53, 55–66

Creating Your High School Resume:
Pages 1–2, 19, 54, and 60–63

Activity 12

Soft and Hard Skills

Objective: Students will learn about soft and hard skills.

Format: Group discussion, individual presentations.

Resources: *Creating Your High School Resume*—pages 60–63.

Ask students to read pages 60–63. Discuss differences between soft and hard skills. Go around the room, asking each student to suggest a soft skill; do the same with hard skills. Let volunteers share their most effective soft and hard skills. If you feel comfortable doing so, elicit students' suggestions as to your soft and hard skills! ■

Activity 13

Working Definitions of Portfolio and Resume

Objective: Students will acquire working definitions of *portfolio* and *resume*.

Format: Individual work, group discussion.

Resources: *Creating Your High School Portfolio*—pages 3–6, *Creating Your High School Resume*—pages 1–2, grade reports, awards, test results, photos, and so on.

Ask students to scan pages 3–6 in *Creating Your High School Portfolio* and pages 1–2 in *Creating Your High School Resume*. Discuss what portfolios and resumes are and why they are important for students. ■

Activity 14

Life Patterns

Objective: Students will look for patterns in their life priorities and values.

Format: Individual work.

Resource: *Creating Your High School Portfolio*—pages 13 and 62.

Allow time for students to read "Personal Information" on page 13. Also, direct students to think about the list at the top of page 62. Next, review life priorities and values previously considered. Much of this will become obvious as students organize the Personal Information section in their portfolios. *Take note of any patterns in all you have accomplished. Do you see many clerical responsibilities? Physical responsibilities? Interpersonal responsibilities?* ■

Activity 15

New Skills Plan

Objective: Students will make a plan to acquire new skills.

Format: Individual work.

Resources: *Creating Your High School Resume*—pages 62–63, paper and pencil.

Ask students to fill out the worksheets on pages 62–63. Ask them to create a simple plan to develop one new skill. ■

Activity 16

Work Experience Charts and Electronic Portfolios

Objective: Students will fill out their work experience chart and discuss electronic portfolios.

Format: Individual work and group discussion.

Resources: *Creating Your High School Portfolio*—pages 27–30 and 55–56, electronic portfolio sample, computer access, PowerPoint, HyperStudio, computer spreadsheet software and disk or paper and pencil.

Allow time for students to quickly read page 55 and fill out "My Paid Employment" on page 56. Also discuss the information about electronic portfolios on pages 27–30. If the resources are available, the work experience data could be part of a database students begin to create with PowerPoint or HyperStudio. Documentation of this work should be included in student portfolios. ■

Activity 17

Student Accomplishments

Objective: Students will consider their accomplishments.

Format: Individual work, interview, and group discussion follow-up.

Resources: *Creating Your High School Portfolio*—pages 16 and 58, paper and pencil.

Allow time for students to read page 16 and complete the worksheet at the bottom of the page. Then ask them to read the top of page 58 and do the activity at the bottom. Direct students to ask a good friend, in or out of school, to write about the student. Compare the results and discuss why others sometimes see us differently than we see ourselves. ■

Activity 18

Self-Description Using Keywords

Objective: Students will write key words describing themselves.

Format: Individual work.

Resources: *Creating Your High School Resume*—page 19, paper and pencil.

Ask students to read "Keywords" on page 19. Discuss with the class what keywords are. Ask a volunteer to name a job. Then ask other students to tell what keywords might be used in a resume for that job. Continue this with 3 or 4 more students. ◼

Activity 19

Essential Skills

Objective: Students will identify essential skills.

Format: Individual work.

Resources: *Creating Your High School Portfolio*—pages 59–61, *Creating Your High School Resume*—pages 60–63, tagboard, markers.

Ask students to read pages 59–61 in *Creating Your High School Portfolio*. Next, compare how the two authors designate skills. Refer to pages 60–63 in *Creating Your High School Resume*. Let students create informational mini-charts on the various kinds of skills. Require each student to prepare his or her own skills list. This skills list can be put into student portfolios. ◼

Activity 20

Skill/Product Analysis

Objective: Students will analyze skills associated with certain products.

Format: Individual work, group discussion.

Resources: *Creating Your High School Portfolio*—pages 59–61, paper and pencil.

Let students have a few minutes to read pages 59–60. Discuss the three types of skills described on page 59. Ask students to choose one skill listed on page 61 that they have. Ask volunteers to share how they demonstrate their skill and what they could put in their portfolio. ■

Activity 21

Want Ads and Needed Skills

Objective: Students will note skills needed for jobs posted in want ads.

Format: Individual work.

Resources: Newspaper job want ads.

Extension activity: Ask students to scan the want ads in newspapers, selecting and cutting out three such ads. The ads should be different in kind. Direct students to make a chart of skills needed for each opening. ■

Activity 22

Interviews

Objective: Students will interview adults regarding their job skills.

Format: Individual work, interview work.

Resources: Relative or neighbor, paper and pencil.

Extension activity: Ask students to interview a parent, relative, or adult neighbor about the skills needed at work. Remind the students to have their skills charts (see Activity 21) with them and to bring up skills the adults might not have thought about as skills in their jobs. ■

Activity 23

Job Skills Worksheet

Objective: Students will complete a worksheet regarding their job skills.

Format: Individual work.

Resources: *Creating Your High School Portfolio*—page 53, *Creating Your High School Resume*—page 54, pencil.

Direct students to fill out the worksheet on page 54 in *Creating Your High School Resume*. Compare it to workbook page 53 in *Creating Your High School Portfolio*. Which do you prefer? Why? ■

Activity 24

Personal Quality Skits

Objective: Students will produce short skits about personal qualities.

Format: Small-group work, skits.

Resources: *Creating Your High School Portfolio*—pages 60–61, box.

Give students a few minutes to read pages 60–61. Refer to the list on page 61. Write each skill on a piece of paper and place in a box. Also include any other skills you think of. Divide the class into small groups. A group representative will draw qualities from the box so each group has two or three qualities. Ask the group to design a two- to three-minute skit demonstrating each of the qualities picked. Qualities could be combined. Let the rest of the class guess which qualities are being portrayed. You may want to talk about appropriateness of skit content and context before starting. ■

Activity 25

Life Change Barriers

Objective: Students will consider barriers to positive life changes.

Format: Individual work.

Resources: *Creating Your High School Portfolio*—page 64, paper and pencil.

Have students read page 64. Ask students to draw on their own papers a box approximately 5 inches x 5 inches. Students should write their names inside the box. On the box perimeter, they should write the major barriers they see keeping them from making important changes in their lives. ■

Activity 26

Life Change Exploration

Objective: Students will explore more fully their life changes through discussion and creative writing.

Format: Individual work, presentation opportunities.

Resources: *Creating Your High School Portfolio*—pages 63–64, paper and pencil or computer access and disk.

Direct students to read page 63, to fill out the worksheet on page 64, and to share it with a friend. Suggest that students compose a song or write a poem about their life changes to date. Students may also wish to predict in song or poem form the future changes they hope to see. Some students will want to read their works aloud; others will not. The finished product may go into portfolios. ■

Activity 27

Overcoming Barriers

Objective: Students will compare and contrast ways that barriers can be overcome.

Format: Group work.

Resources: *Creating Your High School Portfolio*—pages 64–66, paper and pencil.

Ask students to scan pages 64–66. Establish groups with five or six members. Appoint a recorder and ask students to brainstorm ways barriers can be overcome. Compare and contrast lists among groups. ■

Activity 28

Nonwork Experience

Objective: Students will complete a "What I Can Do" checklist.

Format: Individual work.

Resources: *Creating Your High School Portfolio*—page 57, pencil.

The checklist on this page may be filled out and kept for portfolio inclusion. ■

THE JOB FOR YOU IS...?

Overall Objective

The student will examine career interests, begin a networking process with job mentors, and start searching through job resources.

COMPANION TEXTS REFERENCE PAGES

Creating Your High School Portfolio:
Pages 17–18, 53, and 69–79

Creating Your High School Resume:
Pages 10–13, 15–16, 19, 25, 89, 136–138, and 141–147

Activity 29

The Perfect Job

Objective: Students will consider perfect jobs for themselves.

Format: Individual work.

Resources: *Creating Your High School Portfolio*—pages 17–18 and 71–73, computer access and disk or paper and pencil.

Ask students to read "Education and Training" on pages 17–18 and complete the worksheet. Ask students to read page 71 and then complete "My Perfect Job" on pages 72–73. The results may be placed in their portfolios. ■

Activity 30

Analysis of Jobs in 1900 and Today

Objective: Students will examine and analyze jobs that were held in 1900 and compare them to today's jobs.

Format: Independent information gathering.

Resources: Media center, encyclopedias, Internet.

Extension activity: Assign students to gather data on jobs that people held in the year 1900. After each student has a list of ten such jobs, discuss the relevance of each job in today's markets. *Why do jobs change through the years? Will most people your age hold just one job or have only one career in their work life? Explain your thinking.* ■

22

Activity 31

Seeking Job Information

Objective: Using a variety of sources, students will find information about jobs.

Format: Individual work.

Resources: *Creating Your High School Portfolio*—pages 73–76, Web sites.

Ask students to look at pages 74–76. Ask them how they would feel about asking someone to grant them an informational interview. Direct students to read "Sources of Career Information" on pages 73–74. In addition, ask students to locate several sources of online career information. They can do so by searching the Internet with the keywords *career, career planning,* or *jobs.* They can also go to www.jist.com. ■

Activity 32

Mentors and Networking

Objective: Students will learn about mentors and networking.

Format: Individual work, group discussion.

Resource: *Creating Your High School Resume*—pages 10–13 and 15–16.

Assign pages 10–13 and 15–16 for reading. Discuss what a mentor is and how such a person could help your students make wiser career choices. *How is mentoring different from talking to one person about his or her career? Before seeking help from a potential mentor, are there any dos and don'ts to consider?* ■

Activity 33

Career Exploration

Objective: Students will plan an assignment regarding career exploration.

Format: Long-term individual work.

Resources: *Creating Your High School Portfolio*—pages 69–71.

Ask students to look at pages 69–71. Ask them to choose one career and complete the worksheet on pages 70–71. During class, ask students to tell where they got the career research information. ■

Activity 34

Multicareers

Objective: Students will consider the many jobs and careers that individuals hold in their lives.

Format: Individual work.

Resource: *Creating Your High School Portfolio*—page 53, graph paper, paper and pencil.

Direct students to jot down the name of someone in their immediate or extended family. Ask students to list all the jobs that relative has had. This may require data gathering. Discuss findings with all. Graph the results, if applicable. Ask students to complete "Jobs That Interest Me" on page 53. ■

Activity 35
Classified Job Ads

Objective: Students will examine classified job ads.
Format: Individual work, group feedback.
Resources: *Creating Your High School Portfolio*—page 69, classified ad sections of newspaper, paper and pencil.

Ask students to read page 69. Direct students to scan the classified ad section of a major city newspaper. Sunday papers are a ready resource. Let students report what jobs they notice in the classified ads and whether some jobs seem more prevalent than others. Ask students to list five jobs that hold some appeal for them. These lists can be shared with classmates. *Do we have variety in the selections?* ■

Activity 36
Future Job Trends

Objective: Representative students will get information about future job trends.
Format: Individual interview work.
Resources: Think tank, references listed in activity below.

Extension activity: Ask volunteers to get in touch with a think tank (for example, Hudson Institute in Indianapolis, Indiana) and request data and research results regarding future job trends. Also, see the *Young Person's Occupational Outlook Handbook* or *Best Jobs for the 21st Century*. Both books are published by JIST Publishing, Inc. Volunteers should report their findings to the class. ■

Activity 37

Networking and Job Objectives

Objective: Students will find out about networking and write their job objectives.

Format: Individual work, group discussion, and pairs work.

Resources: *Creating Your High School Resume*—pages 15–16 and 89, paper and pencil.

Ask students to read the information about networking. Discuss the difference between a mentor and a person who is in one's network. Next, ask students to talk with a partner about each other's job objectives. Allow several minutes for this exchange. Ask students to put their job objectives in writing and include these objectives in their portfolios. ■

Activity 38

Networking Template

Objective: Students will fill out a networking template.

Format: Individual work and group discussion.

Resources: *Creating Your High School Portfolio*—pages 77–79, paper and pencil or computer software such as PowerPoint.

Ask students to read "Networking" on pages 77–78. Discuss Figure 1 on page 78. Give students some class time to start filling in information about their own networks, using Figure 2 on page 79. Assign a due date for a finished product. Remind students that their network will change as they meet new contacts through daily activities. Personal network maps should be put into portfolios. ■

© JIST Works

Activity 39

Job Leads

Objective: Students will learn about handling job leads.
Format: Individual work, pairs work, and presentations.
Resources: *Creating Your High School Resume*—pages 136–138, telephone model, paper and pencil.

These pages show students how to handle job leads, whether on the telephone, in classified ads, or on the Internet. Ask students to read the information on job leads using the telephone. Talk about content and then give pairs of students several minutes to create a telephone script for contacting a job lead. The script should be no more than two minutes. Give pairs an opportunity to present their script to the class. If time permits, do a phone lead example and make it horrendous! Critique the interchanges. A copy of a personalized, effective telephone script should go into their portfolios. ■

Activity 40

Keywords in Job Ads

Objective: Students will recognize keywords in job ads.
Format: Individual work, group discussion.
Resources: *Creating Your High School Resume*—pages 19 and 25, newspaper classified job ads, highlighters.

Assign pages 19 and 25 as reading. Next, either assign students to collect newspaper classified job ads to discuss later, or hand out previously collected newspaper classified job ads to students. Give students a few minutes to highlight keywords in five ads. Ask students if there are similarities in keywords. Discuss keywords the class finds. List the keywords on the board. Talk about the meaning of keywords on the list. ■

Activity 41

Cold Calling for a Job

Objective: Students will practice cold calling for a job.

Format: Individual work.

Resources: *Creating Your High School Resume*—pages 141–142, telephone model, paper and pencil.

Go over steps for cold calling a person about a job. Assign each student to write a general "cold call" script and to hand in the written product. Talk about how one prepares for a cold call, even before the actual call is made. Add cold call tips to the portfolio. ■

Activity 42

Internet Job Opportunities

Objective: Students will explore job opportunities on the Internet.

Format: Individual work or group demonstration.

Resources: *Creating Your High School Resume*—pages 142–147, computer lab or class computer, Internet access.

Direct students to read pages 142–147. Take students to a computer lab or demonstrate on the computer(s) that you have available for Internet access. If necessary, go over basics about Internet use and explain search engines (AltaVista, Lycos, Excite, Yahoo!, and so on). Try out some of the Web sites. If enough computers are available, direct each student to find three sites that list jobs of interest to them. If you need to pair students because of limited computers, do so. Or, as a class demonstration, you can show the potential the Internet has for job hunting! ■

EXPLORING YOUR OPTIONS

Overall Objective

The student will examine available educational opportunities, find out about the cost of such opportunities, and start developing a resume and portfolio.

COMPANION TEXTS REFERENCE PAGES

Creating Your High School Portfolio:
Pages 62, 98–99, and 101–125

Creating Your High School Resume:
Pages 2–4, 18–24, 27–29, 31–32, 101–129, and 132–134

Activity 43

Available, Appealing Jobs

Objective: Students will consider the types of available jobs that appeal to them.

Format: Group discussion.

Resources: *Creating Your High School Resume*—pages 132–134, computer access and disk or pencil and paper.

With your students, skim job possibilities on these pages. *Which possibilities attract your attention the most? Why?* Ask students to write an essay about the areas that appeal to them. Remind students of essay components: opener, body of content, summary. Remember, an essay is not a list! A copy of the final product should go into their portfolios. ■

Activity 44

Entry- and 10-Year-Level Salaries Comparison

Objective: Students will compare entry- and 10-year-level salaries of five occupations.

Format: Individual work, information gathering.

Resources: *Creating Your High School Portfolio*—pages 98–99, reference books, Internet, Department of Labor statistics, personal interview, paper and pencil.

Extension activity: Refer to "Does Education Pay Off?" on pages 98–99. Ask your students to check in various references for the salaries of five occupations that they'd like to hold. Ask them to look at entry pay and again at 10-year salaries for those same jobs. This work will involve some data gathering, either on the Internet, on the telephone, by personal interview, or from a print resource. If they use a print resource, remind students to get the very latest figures possible. Set appropriate due dates for this work. ■

Activity 45

Facts About the Top U.S. Jobs

Objective:	Students will study and learn facts about the top jobs in the U.S.
Format:	Individual work, group discussion.
Resources:	*Creating Your High School Portfolio*—pages 62 and 101–106, paper and pencil.

Ask students to list the ten most appealing jobs they know of. Allow two minutes. Discuss briefly. Then, encourage students to use the data on pages 101–106 to rank their 10 jobs by education/training (most to least required) and by earnings (most to least earned). Ask students if there are any surprises about their choices as related to earnings and education. Direct attention to page 62 as a reminder that "Education and Training" is one important portfolio section. ∎

Activity 46

Salary Comparisons of the Top U.S. Jobs

Objective:	Students will figure percentages of low, average, high, and very high wages of the top jobs in U.S.
Format:	Individual work, group work.
Resource:	*Creating Your High School Portfolio*—pages 101–106.

Extension activity: Try this math exercise! Ask your students to review the data on pages 101–106 and to determine what percentage of the occupations listed earns low wages. Do the same for average wages, high wages, and very high wages. You may need to review how to calculate percentages before assigning this exercise. ∎

Activity 47

Interviewing Others About Their Jobs

Objective: Students will interview five people about their jobs.

Format: Individual work, interviews.

Resources: *Creating Your High School Portfolio*—page 107, roundtable for discussion, paper and pencil.

Ask students to read "Go to the Experts" on page 107. Ask them to talk with five people about their work and to fill in the other worksheet on page 107. (Use blank sheets of paper as needed.) Decide on an appropriate due date. Hold a roundtable discussion regarding interview findings. ■

Activity 48

Job Training Opportunities Poster

Objective: Students will create a poster of job training opportunities.

Format: Individual work.

Resources: *Creating Your High School Portfolio*—page 108, related occupational information books, poster board, and markers.

Ask students to read page 108 and to find four on-the-job training opportunities through the Internet, classified ads, and related job listing references (for example, *Best Jobs for the 21st Century, Young Person's Occupational Outlook Handbook,* and *Occupational Outlook Handbook*). Finally, give students time to create an appealing poster showing on-the-job training opportunities. Posters should show job locations, telephone numbers, and pertinent information about each job. ■

Activity 49

Apprenticeships

Objective: Students will compare on-the-job training with apprenticeships.

Format: Individual work.

Resources: *Creating Your High School Portfolio*—pages 108–111, related occupational listing books, paper and pencil.

Direct students to read "Apprenticeships" on pages 109–110. Review page 108. Next ask them to write concise paragraphs comparing on-the-job training with apprenticeships. Elicit as many contrasts and similarities between the two as possible. If information is relevant to the job future of students, advise that they include the paragraphs in their portfolios. ■

Activity 50

Advantages and Disadvantages of Trade or Technical Schools

Objective: Students will list advantages and disadvantages of trade or technical schools.

Format: Pairs work or small-group discussion.

Resources: *Creating Your High School Portfolio*—pages 112–113, chart paper, markers.

Allow pairs or small groups to read pages 112–113. Hand each pair or group a piece of chart paper and marker. Give students about five minutes for discussion and for the listing of trade or technical school advantages and disadvantages. If the information is relevant to the job future of students, advise that they include a written summary in their portfolios. ■

Activity 51

Local College and University Degree Programs

Objective: Students will check out local and state colleges and universities regarding degrees and programs offered, as well as their associated costs. They will also explore available military service training and benefits. (See Activity 52 for students whose post–high school plans do not include university or military training.)

Format: Teamwork, group discussion.

Resources: *Creating Your High School Portfolio*—pages 114–119, local college and university course descriptions, registrars, military services recruiting personnel, and so on.

Direct students to read pages 114, 116, and 118. Divide students into fact-finding teams. Assign each team a local state college or university or a military service organization. Advise teams to contact their source about degrees and training offered. Teams should use the worksheets on pages 115, 117, and 119. Upon completion of these contacts, hold team presentations of their findings. Compare the economic value of associate and bachelor's degrees. Discuss factors that help determine which schools and training individuals select.

See Activity 52 for students who are not interested in higher education or serving in the military. The results of either of these information searches, if applicable to future jobs of students, should be included in their portfolios. ■

Activity 52

Employment Opportunities After High School

Objective: Students will gather information regarding post–high school employment opportunities.

Format: Individual work, group discussion.

Resources: *Creating Your High School Portfolio*—pages 108–113, personnel directors, workers, and so on.

Activity 51 involved students who may be interested in higher education or military service. Activity 52 is for those who are not. Ask these students to contact a business personnel director or current job holder in a field that interests them, or a trade or technical school representative. Students should interview appropriate persons regarding on-the-job training, apprenticeship, or trade and technical schools. Students may use pages 108–113 to obtain information. Direct this group to gather for a discussion of their findings and concerns. Any information relevant to the future jobs of any students should be included in their portfolios. ▪

Activity 53

Personal Financial Resources

Objective: Students will consider their own financial resources and estimated costs of higher education or job training.

Format: Individual work.

Resources: *Creating Your High School Portfolio*—page 121, family or guardian.

Ask students to review the worksheet on page 121 with you. Discuss the process of obtaining the information needed to complete such a form. Ask each student to select a college/university, a military service, or a job training opportunity and complete the worksheet. Of course, this information is strictly confidential. You may not need to collect the papers; simply check off that the work was done. This completed worksheet should be added to student portfolios. ▪

Activity 54

Sources of Financial Aid

Objective: The students will learn about sources of financial aid, including their state's financial aid program.

Format: Teamwork, group discussion.

Resource: *Creating Your High School Portfolio*—pages 120–121.

Assign to each team of several students one of the six sources of federal financial assistance on pages 120–121. Ask each group to find out pertinent facts about those sources. Discuss with students who they might contact for additional information on financial aid. Allow several days for this work and then discuss and compare findings. Pertinent information regarding any student's future education and training should be included in that person's portfolio. ■

Activity 55

Planning High School Courses for Job Success

Objective: Students will plan high school courses that will support future job success.

Format: Individual work.

Resources: *Creating Your High School Portfolio*—pages 122–125, high school counselor, teacher, parent(s) or guardian(s).

Direct students to consider the junior- and senior-year classes that will prepare them for their chosen careers and to plan ahead for these years. The worksheets on pages 122–125, when applicable, should be added to the student portfolios. ■

Activity 56
Types of Resumes

Objective:	Students will learn about various types of resumes.
Format:	Individual, pairs work, group discussion.
Resources:	*Creating Your High School Resume*—pages 2–4, 18–21, 23–24, 27–29, 31–32, paper and pencil.

Ask students to read pages 2–4. Discuss the purpose and importance of resumes and how these documents will grow and change as the students mature. Ask students to read pages 18–21. Allow five minutes for them to write what they remember about the basic resume types. Next, direct students to study actual resumes on pages 23–24, 27–29, 31–32. Ask students to pay special attention to Emily Thompson's resumes on pages 23–24. Discuss the differences in the two resumes. ■

Activity 57
Typical Chronological Resume

Objective:	Students will study a typical chronological resume.
Format:	Individual work.
Resources:	*Creating Your High School Resume*—pages 20–22 and 24, evidence of school honors, recognitions, work experience, and so on.

Ask students to read pages 20–22 and 24. Advise students who plan to attend a college or university in preparation for a chosen career to begin to collect similar information and items (for example, honors and recognition evidence, published writings, computer skills listing, and so on). Of course, these pieces of evidence should be housed in their portfolios until resumes are formulated. ■

Activity 58

Targeted Resumes

Objective: Students will study sample targeted resumes.
Format: Individual work.
Resources: *Creating Your High School Resume*—pages 19–20 and 22–23, evidence of school honors, recognitions, work experience, and so on.

Ask students to read pages 19–20 and 22–23. Advise students who plan to seek jobs, internships, and service learning experiences to begin to collect similar information and items (for example, honors and recognition evidence, published writings, computer skills listing, and so on). Of course, these pieces of evidence should be housed in their portfolios until resumes are formulated. ■

Activity 59

Resume Case Studies

Objective: Students will examine resume case studies.
Format: Pairs work, group discussion.
Resources: *Creating Your High School Resume*—pages 101–129.

Assign the case studies to pairs of students. Ask pairs to discuss each of their case studies. Allow time for reading and discussing the case studies. Hold class discussion over the last several minutes for wrap-up. ■

38

MAKING IT HAPPEN!

Overall Objective

The student will put together an action plan for getting a job in a chosen career area.

COMPANION TEXTS REFERENCE PAGES

Creating Your High School Portfolio:
Pages 3–6, 15, 18, 55, 95–96, 127–130, 130–131, 132–134, 134–136, 137–138, 138–141, 145–146, and 149

Creating Your High School Resume:
Pages 5–17, 35–56, 73–80, 81–83, 83–84, 86–94, 95–96, 97–98, and 148–150

Activity 60

Action Plan for Reaching a Job or Career Goal

Objective: Students will fill out an overall action plan for reaching a job or career goal.

Format: Individual work.

Resources: *Creating Your High School Portfolio*—pages 15 and 95–96, individual student portfolios, computer access and disk or paper and pencil.

Ask students to read "Introduction and Personal Reflections" on page 15. Allow time for them to complete the worksheet at the bottom of the page. Direct students to read "Put Together a Plan" on page 95, to review their own portfolio contents, and to consider an overall action plan for reaching a job or career goal. Of course, many students will have already begun such a journey. Each student should complete the worksheet on page 96 or prepare a similar document on disk. Add this product to student portfolios with your signature. *How does writing such a plan help us to focus on the commitment aspect of goal attainment?* ■

Activity 61

Job Reference Sources

Objective: Students will examine various job reference sources.

Format: Individual work, group discussion.

Resource: *Creating Your High School Portfolio*—pages 18 and 55.

Ask students to look at "People's Opinions" on page 18 and complete the worksheet there. Have students read the fifth paragraph down on page 55 (It starts with "Also, for each job....") Discuss. *Why are family members not considered reliable references when compared to teachers, former employers, and others who have direct knowledge of one's skills and strengths as an employee or worker?* ■

Activity 62

Mock Job Inquiry Calls, Interview Setups, and Job Interviews

Objective:	Students will observe and take part in pretend job inquiry calls, interview setups, and job interviews.
Format:	Skit demonstrations.
Resources:	*Creating Your High School Portfolio*—pages 127–130, skit descriptions for two telephone calls to set up job interviews, for two calls to make job inquiries, and for two job interviews.

Don't prepare word-for-word scripts, but do set parameters or create template frameworks for each mock inquiry call and interview before soliciting student volunteers. You should take the role of potential employer in each scene. Students will take part in and observe others in demonstration scenes: calling for an interview, making a job inquiry, taking part in a job interview. After your students have done this, ask them to read "Job Applications" on pages 127–128. Ask them to fill out "My Job Application Fact Sheet" on pages 128–130. Repeat the pretend calls/interviews, but this time direct the students to use their fact sheets during the process. When completed, review whether the fact sheets had a positive or negative influence during the mock scenes. ■

Activity 63

Sample Resume Examinations

Objective:	Students will examine several resume examples.
Format:	Individual work and group discussion.
Resources:	*Creating Your High School Portfolio*—pages 130–131, *Creating Your High School Resume*—pages 73–80.

Ask students to read pages 130–131 in *Creating Your High School Portfolio* and pages 76–77 and 79–80 in *Creating Your High School Resume*. Look at the various resumes on pages 73–75 and 78 in *Creating Your High School Resume*. Discuss the different resume styles and what appeals to your students. *Can the style or appearance of a resume have an effect on a potential employer?* ■

Activity 64

Resume Honors and Awards

Objective:	Students will list honors and awards.
Format:	Individual work.
Resources:	*Creating Your High School Resume*—pages 40–41, computer access and disk.

Direct students to see sample listings on page 40 in *Creating Your High School Resume*, and then ask them to compose their own lists. Use the worksheet on page 41 as you direct their writing. This may be a two-period assignment because your students may need to do some school or home data gathering before compiling their lists. A computer list looks more professional than a handwritten one. This product should go into the student portfolio. ■

Activity 65

Resume Activities

Objective: Students will record all their high school activities.

Format: Individual work, class discussion.

Resource: *Creating Your High School Resume*—page 42.

Ask students to read the section on activities on page 42 in *Creating Your High School Resume*. Discuss the importance of such experiences to future employers. Using the worksheet on page 42, guide students as they list all of their high school activities. Talk about the importance of organization in such a listing; point out that a *combined* honors/activities resume section may be an appropriate format. As in Activity 64, you may need to spread this activity over two periods so your students can collect the data needed for such listings. The final product should be put into the student portfolio. ■

Activity 66

Workshops, Seminars, and Related Learning Programs

Objective: Students will consider and record workshops, seminars, and related programs they attended.

Format: Individual work, class discussion.

Resources: *Creating Your High School Resume*—pages 43–51, teachers, family, workshop and seminar leaders, and so on.

Ask students to read pages 43–51 in *Creating Your High School Resume*. Next, give a class discussion opportunity for examples of workshops, seminars, work-study, or tech-prep programs that students have attended. Talk about the value of furthering one's knowledge and how additional information and training can create future job opportunities. Have students record their own learning and training workshop experiences. The final product should go into student portfolios. ■

Activity 67

Work Experience

Objective: Students will record their own work experience
                     to date.
Format: Individual work, small-group work.
Resources: *Creating Your High School Resume*—pages
                     51–54, past employers.

Discuss "Work Experience" in *Creating Your High School Resume* on pages
51–54. Ask small groups of three or four to prioritize the work experience
factors all employers look for in potential workers. Allow 15 minutes for
this exercise and then gather group decisions and hold a class discussion
about findings. Finally, ask your students to list their own part-time and
full-time positions, including the name of each employer, title of position
held, and employment dates. Your students may need to do some fact
finding before completing this list. Extend the assignment to the next
period for fact gathering. The final product should go into the student
portfolio. ■

Activity 68

Portfolio Content Update

Objective: Students will review and update their portfolio
                     contents.
Format: Individual work.
Resources: Students, teachers, family, past employers,
                     student portfolios.

Extension activity: Before this class period, ask students to bring their
portfolios to class for review and update. If the portfolios are electronic,
students should bring their disks and related documentation. Allow time
for organization and self-assessment of portfolio contents. Encourage
students to share their portfolios with a class friend. ■

Activity 69

Resume Worksheet Completion

Objective: Students will complete a resume worksheet.
Format: Individual work, group discussion.
Resources: *Creating Your High School Portfolio*—pages 132–133, portfolios, computer access and disk or paper and pencil.

Direct students to complete "My Resume Worksheet" on pages 132–133 of *Creating Your High School Portfolio.* Employment history will require dates. Advise students to find this specific information, much of which is already in their portfolios. As a class, talk about the necessity of keeping track of skills, accomplishments, and qualifications because these things become part of their lives. After all, it is these things that open job opportunity doors! Add the final product to the portfolios. ■

Activity 70

Grammar in Resume Writing

Objective: Students will work on the grammar in resume writing.
Format: Individual work.
Resources: *Creating Your High School Resume*—pages 81–83; a sample of a previously created, poorly written resume; computer access and disk.

Ask students to read pages 81–83. Next, hand out a previously created, poorly written resume. Ask students to critique the resume and to re-create an appropriate one using the same information. ■

Activity 71

Two Resumes

Objective: Students will create two resumes.

Format: Individual work.

Resources: *Creating Your High School Resume*—pages 35–56 and 83–84, computer access and disk.

This assignment will take more than one period. Students should read pages 83–84. Next, they should fill out pertinent worksheets from Chapter 3 (pages 35–56). In class, ask students to create a resume for a job they'd like to have today and to create another for a job they'd like to have five to ten years in the future. Preferably, this work can be done on disks and saved for changes later. Any data organized from this lesson should be included in student portfolios. ■

Activity 72

Resume Cover Letters

Objective: Students will prepare cover letters for their resumes.

Format: Individual work, group discussion.

Resources: *Creating Your High School Portfolio*—pages 134–136, *Creating Your High School Resume*—pages 86–94, computer access, disk, personnel director of a school system or a local business.

Direct students to read pages 134–136 in *Creating Your High School Portfolio* and pages 86–94 in *Creating Your High School Resume*. Discuss. Give students time to compose and print out their cover letters for the two jobs sought in Activity 71. Invite your school system's personnel director or a personnel director from a business to talk about the importance of first impressions. Ask them to critique cover letters (unnamed) written by the class to see if the letters would make a good first impression. ■

Activity 73

Refining Cover Letters

Objective: Students will refine their cover letters based on objective criticism from classmates.

Format: Individual work.

Resources: *Creating Your High School Resume*—pages 86–94, computer access and disk.

Direct students to study pages 86–94 and then to revise their two cover letters. The final letters could be assessed by one other student and by you. Copies of final letters should be included in student portfolios. ■

Activity 74

Resume Uses

Objective: Students will discover the several uses for their resumes.

Format: Individual work, group discussion.

Resources: *Creating Your High School Resume*—pages 5–17, paper and pencil.

Ask students to read pages 5–17. Discuss with the class the many uses of a resume. Solicit personal experiences from students, if applicable. Share your own past experiences, too! ■

Activity 75

Importance of References

Objective:	Students will consider the importance of references.
Format:	Individual work.
Resources:	*Creating Your High School Resume*—pages 95–96, paper and pencil.

Assign students pages 95–96 as reading and then ask them to think of people who might be good references for their job searches. Advise students to get permission from at least three possible references and then to complete the worksheet on page 96. Students should include this finished information in their portfolios. ■

Activity 76

Thank-You Letter Critiques and Writing

Objective:	Students will critique and write thank-you letters.
Format:	Individual work, pairs work.
Resources:	*Creating Your High School Resume*—pages 97–98, thank-you letter test.

Direct students to critique sample thank-you letters that you have previously acquired or written. Share several sample thank-you letters with your students, either on the overhead projector, with a visual presenter, or in paper copy form for each student. As a class or individually, go over each letter, making suggestions for its improvement. You might want to assess your students' letter-writing skills at this time with a "test" letter for them to critique. The finished test letter could be placed in the student portfolio. ■

Activity 77

Telephone Job Inquiry Practice

Objective: Students will practice telephone job inquiries.

Format: Small-group work, presentations, and group discussion.

Resources: *Creating Your High School Portfolio*—pages 137–138, paper and pencil.

Ask students to read "Employer Contacts" on pages 137–138. Divide students into groups of three or four. Set aside half of the class period for students to create a negative and a positive telephone job inquiry. Encourage students to use the guidelines on page 137 and the telephone script on page 138 when scripting the positive inquiry. On the other hand, advise groups to botch up the negative effort with drama and errors! Use the second half of the class period for presentations. Allow a few minutes for discussion of results. Ask each student to complete a positive, final telephone inquiry script and place it in the student portfolio. ■

Activity 78

Job Interview Preparation and Dramatizations

Objective: Students will prepare and dramatize job interviews.

Format: Individual work, class discussion, and group presentations.

Resources: *Creating Your High School Portfolio*—pages 138–141, *Creating Your High School Resume*—pages 148–150, paper and pencil.

Direct students to read pages 138–141 in *Creating Your High School Portfolio* and pages 148–150 in *Creating Your High School Resume*. Discuss the information as a class. Next, pair students and ask each pair to work on a mock interview scenario for the next class period. All interview tips should be followed, including the "dress" for such a meeting. ■

Activity 79

The First 10 Days in a New Job

Objective: Students will consider the first days in a new job.

Format: Individual work, class discussion, and pairs work.

Resources: *Creating Your High School Portfolio*—pages 145–146, volunteer parents of students, paper and pencil, markers, poster board.

Ask students to seek parents who will volunteer to come to the next class and discuss their first few weeks on any new job they've held in the past. Prior to the parents' visitation, students should read page 145 in *Creating Your High School Portfolio* and look at the checklist on page 146. Students should prepare several questions for their guests. Following this class, allow small groups of students to make posters showing the basic areas that are critical for job success. The checklist on page 146 could be added to the students' portfolios. ■

Activity 80

Writing About a New Job

Objective: Students will write about the first days of a new job.

Format: Individual work, class discussion.

Resources: *Creating Your High School Portfolio*—page 145, computer access and disk or paper and pencil.

Ask students to review the first paragraph under "Keep Your New Job" on page 145. Students will write a clear, concise essay about why the first few days of a new job are called a "honeymoon." ■

Activity 81

Growing on the Job

Objective: Students will write about growing on the job.
Format: Individual work, class discussion.
Resources: *Creating Your High School Portfolio*—pages 147–148, computer access and disk or paper and pencil.

Students will write a paper about growing on the job and present it to the class. There should be individual, critical thinking. Although the list on page 147 is an excellent one, students' papers must show some originality of thought. The "My Areas for Growth" checklist on page 148 should be included in the student portfolios. ■

Activity 82

Portfolio Review and Assessment

Objective: Students will review and assess their portfolios.
Format: Individual work, class discussion, or small-group work.
Resources: *Creating Your High School Portfolio*—pages 3–6, and 149, student portfolios.

Divide students into four small groups. Assign each group one page—page 3, 4, 5, or 6. Allow groups to discuss the information on their pages. Ask each group to tell the class something that was important or new. Also, students will bring their portfolios to class to review and assess. Some reorganization may be necessary. Allow ample time for this process. Let students share one or more items from their portfolios with the class. The students may ask questions, too. Refer students to page 149 and discuss the fact that career planning is an ongoing process. ■

Activity Cross-References for Using the Companion Texts Sequentially

If you wish to use *Creating Your High School Portfolio* and *Creating Your High School Resume* sequentially, the following two tables will help. The page numbers from the two texts are listed in sequence and cross-referenced with the Part I activity numbers.

TABLE 1

CORRELATION BETWEEN *CREATING YOUR HIGH SCHOOL PORTFOLIO* AND PART I ACTIVITIES

Creating Your High School Portfolio Page(s)	Part I Activity Number(s)	Part I Page Number(s)
3–6	13, 82	12, 51
7–8	10	9
9	2, 10	5, 9
10–11	2	5
13	14	13
14	1	5
15	1, 60	5, 40
16	17	14
17	29	22
18	29, 61	22, 40
27–30	16	14
33–34	1, 11	5, 10
35	1, 2	5
36	2	5
38–41	3	6
42	3, 5	6–7
43–47	3, 6	6–7
48	3, 6–7	6–8
49	7	8
50	8, 10	8–9
51	8	8
52	11	10
53	11, 23, 34	10, 17, 24
55	16, 61	14, 40
56	16	14
57	28	20

© JIST Works

Creating Your High School Portfolio Page(s)	Part I Activity Number(s)	Part I Page Number(s)
58	17	14
59	19–20	15–16
60	19–20, 24	15–16, 18
61	19–20, 24	15–16, 18
62	14, 45	13, 31
63	26	19
64	25–27	18–19
65–66	27	19
69	33, 35	24–25
70	33	24
71	29, 33	22, 24
72	29	22
73	29, 31	22–23
74–76	31	23
77–79	38	26
95–96	60	40
98–99	44	30
101–106	45–46	31
107	47	32
108	48–49, 52	32–33, 35
109–111	49, 52	33, 35
112–113	50, 52	33, 35
114–119	51	34
120	54	36
121	53–54	35–36
122–125	55	36
127–130	62	41
130–131	63	42
132–133	69	45
134–136	72	46
137	77	49
138	77–78	49
139–141	78	49
145	79–80	50
146	79	50
147–148	81	51
149	82	51

TABLE 2

CORRELATION BETWEEN *CREATING YOUR HIGH SCHOOL RESUME* AND PART I ACTIVITIES

Creating Your High School Resume Page(s)	Part I Activity Number(s)	Part I Page Number(s)
1–2	13	12
2–4	56	37
5–9	74	47
10–13	32, 74	23, 47
14	74	47
15–16	32, 37, 74	23, 26, 47
17	74	47
18	56	37
19	18, 40, 56, 58	15, 27, 37–38
20	56, 58	37–38
21	56–57	37
22	57–58	37–38
23	56, 58	37–38
24	56–57	37
25	40	27
27–29, 31–32	56	37
35–39	71	46
40–41	64, 71	42, 46
42	65, 71	43, 46
43–50	66, 71	43, 46
51	66–67, 71	43–44, 46
52–53	67, 71	44, 46
54	23, 67, 71	17, 44, 46
55–56	71	46
60–61	12, 19	12, 15
62	12, 14–15, 19	12–13, 15
63	12, 15, 19	12–13, 15
73–80	63	42
81–82	70	45
83	70–71	45–46
84	71	46
86–88	72, 73	46–47
89	37, 72, 73	26, 46–47
90–94	72, 73	46–47
95–96	75	48
97–98	76	48
101–129	59	38
132–134	43	30
136–138	39	27
141	41	28
142	41–42	28
143–147	42	28
148–150	78	49

PART II

Teaching Hints and Transparency Masters
for
Creating Your High School Portfolio

Compiled by JIST Editors

Overview

The following tips and transparency masters can be used to lead your students through all or part of *Creating Your High School Portfolio*. The part and page numbers under each transparency master refer to those in *Creating Your High School Portfolio*. It would be best for students to read each part of the book before you cover it in class.

Transparency 1: Table of Contents

Ask students to glance through each chapter of the workbook to see what the general content of that chapter is. Emphasize each point on Transparency 1.

Transparency 2: Understanding Portfolios

Some of your students will already know what a portfolio is and how a portfolio can help them. Many will not. Workbook pages 3–5 will reinforce what students already know and give them a good foundation for creating their portfolio. After students have read pages 3–5 and completed the worksheets, ask them to name points that are new to them.

Transparency 3: Self-Exploration

Explain to students that self-exploration is one of the hidden benefits of creating a portfolio. Students will not be able to put together and organize their portfolios if they don't have information about themselves. Use Transparency 3 to reinforce the idea of organizing a portfolio around self-exploration.

Transparency 4: Information on Who You Are

Form five teams. Assign each team one of the five points on Transparency 4. Allow time for teams to meet and discuss workbook pages 32–42. Ask each team to choose a representative to explain what the group discovered. Ask students to complete workbook pages 32–42. Ask students to explain how each worksheet relates to the students' awareness of who they are.

Transparency 5: Your Health Affects What You Do with Your Life and Career

Allow time for students to complete workbook pages 43–48. Discuss each item on Transparency 5. Brainstorm the effects of poor physical or emotional health on a person's life and career. Encourage students to give specific examples. As students look at Transparency 5, let volunteers name the area of physical or emotional health that is hardest for them. Ask other class members to suggest ways each volunteer could improve his or her health.

Transparency 6: Balance Life Roles

Reveal each bulleted item on Transparency 6. Allow time for students to write down one life role they have. Follow the same procedure for the second bulleted item. Reveal the third point on Transparency 6 and ask students to describe how theses might affect a student's education and career choices.

Transparency 7: Your Career Interests

Ask students to look at the worksheet "My Career Interests" on workbook pages 52–53. One by one, reveal the points on Transparency 7. For each point, ask students to raise their hands if that is a type of career they are interested in. For each career interest, allow volunteers to tell what appeals to them about a job in that career interest group.

Transparency 8: What You Can Do

Help students see that everyone can do something–even if it seems like a minor thing. Use Transparency 8 and workbook pages 54–62. Help students realize that they have things they can do. They may also have weak areas. Ask students to name paid jobs they know about. Ask them to name nonwork activities for students. Ask them what a high school student can accomplishment. Ask them to describe skills and attributes a student may have.

Transparency 9: Identify Your Skills

Form three teams. Give each team a large piece of paper. Show Transparency 9. Ask teams to look at workbook pages 59–61. Assign one team each to the three types of skills described in those pages. Encourage teams to think of as many skills as they can in the category they were assigned. Teams should write these skills on their papers and then tape them to the wall. Discuss.

Transparency 10: Challenges and Realities

One by one, reveal the items listed on Transparency 10 and ask students to respond aloud to each item. Next, allow time for students to look at or review workbook pages 63–66. Ask students to describe how the information on those pages might change the responses they gave earlier.

Transparency 11: Explore Career Options

Allow time for a few comments from students about their perfect jobs. Use Transparency 11. Ask students which characteristic of a job would be most important to them. For example, if they found a good job that was perfect in most ways, but that was located somewhere they wouldn't want to live, would they accept the job?

Transparency 12: Explore Different Careers and Gather Information About Specific Jobs

Ask students to review or complete workbook pages 69–71. Show the top part of Transparency 12. Ask two volunteers to role-play an informational interview. One person will be the student and one person will be someone in a career that interests the student. When the two students finish, discuss the role-play situation. Call for class feedback. Show the bottom part of Transparency 12. Briefly discuss each point. Ask students to complete workbook page 92.

Transparency 13: Training and Education Options

Refer to workbook pages 79–81. Ask students to complete the worksheet on page 81. Remind them that the training and education they need will depend on the job they choose and the career goals they set. Look at workbook pages 108–119. Ask students to identify types of education and training they might not have thought of previously.

Transparency 14: Check Out Schools

Ask students to complete one of the worksheets on workbook pages 112–121. Encourage students to think about the many options available to them. Help them understand the importance of getting good information about schools before enrolling.

Transparency 15: Apply for a Job

Form four teams of students. Assign the following topics to each team: job applications (workbook pages 127–130); resumes (pages 130–133); cover letters (pages 134–136); or employer contacts (pages 137–138). Allow teams a few minutes to discuss the topics they are assigned, and then let them share with the class.

Transparency 16: Prepare for Interviews

Role-play a job interview. Choose one volunteer to serve as an employer. You will be the person interviewing for a job. Ask students to refer to workbook pages 138–141 and to evaluate your interview.

Transparency 17: Keep Your New Job

Ask students to tell why each point on Transparency 17 is important. Ask them to describe a work situation where an employee does not have one of these characteristics.

Transparency 18: Grow on the Job

Allow time for students to complete or review the worksheet on workbook page 148. Uncover the points in Transparency 18 one at a time. Discuss.

Creating Your High School Portfolio

Table of Contents

Part One: Creating a Portfolio

Part Two: Understanding Yourself

Part Three: Reaching Your Career Goals

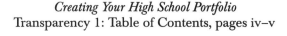

Understanding Portfolios

- Definition

- Benefits

- Goals

- Organization

Self-Exploration

- Personal Information

- Values

- Introduction and Personal Reflections

- Accomplishments and Job History

- Skills and Attributes

- Education and Training

- People's Opinions

Information on Who You Are

- What do you stand for? Name two things that are important to you.

- What is your learning style? Explain how you best learn something new.

- What is your personality style? Describe how you act in different situations.

- What is your risk-taking style? Explain how you feel about starting something new.

- What is your time-management style? Name two ways you manage time.

Creating Your High School Portfolio
Transparency 4: Part Two, pages 32–42

Your Health Affects What You Do with Your Life and Career

- Dealing with stress

- Staying physically healthy

  - Eat well
  - Be physically active

- Find emotional support

- Use effective coping methods

Balance Life Roles

- What are your roles in life?
  Student, sibling, friend?

- What shapes your life roles?
  Family, gender, where you grew up?

- How will your roles affect your
  education and career choices?

Creating Your High School Portfolio
Transparency 6: Part Two, pages 48–51

Your Career Interests

- Arts, Entertainment, and Media
- Science, Math, and Engineering
- Plants and Animals
- Law, Law Enforcement, and Public Safety
- Mechanics, Installers, and Repairers
- Construction, Mining, and Drilling
- Transportation
- Industrial Production
- Business Detail
- Sales and Marketing
- Recreation, Travel, and Other Services
- Education and Social Service
- General Management and Support
- Medical and Health Services

What You Can Do

Look at

- Your work experience

- Your home, leisure, and community activities

- Your accomplishments

- Your skills and attributes

Identify Your Skills

Major Types of Skills

- **Self-management skills:** flexibility, friendliness, punctuality

- **Transferable skills:** meeting deadlines, writing clearly

- **Job-related skills:** driving a truck, preparing a teaching plan

Challenges and Realities

- Name some changes that have happened to you

- Name some changes that will happen to you after high school

- Explain what you've learned from change

- Discuss how you handle change

- Describe some barriers to change

68

Explore Career Options

Your Ideal Job:

- Location

- Work site

- Tasks and responsibilities

- Coworkers

Explore Different Careers

- Informational interviews

- Job shadowing

- Career information software and Web sites

- Career resource centers

- Networking

Gather Information About Specific Jobs

- Nature of the work

- Training/education required

- Working conditions

- Advancement potential

- How well a job matches your interests and skills

Training and Education Options

- On-the-job training

- Apprenticeships

- Trade or technical school

- Associate degree

- Bachelor's degree

- Military training

What kind of education or training do you need for the career you want?

Creating Your High School Portfolio
Transparency 13: Part Three, pages 79–81, 108–119

Check Out Schools

- Get employers' viewpoints

- Comparison shop

- Look at program requirements and catalogs

- Look at tuition and fees

- Find out about accreditation

- Ask about financial aid and tuition assistance

Apply for a Job

- Job applications

- Resumes

- Cover letters

- Employer contacts

Prepare for Interviews

- Find out about the employer

- Practice the interview

- Prepare answers to commonly asked questions

- Follow up with a note or phone call

Keep Your New Job

- ● Be dependable and reliable

- ● Be punctual

- ● Be productive in both quality and quantity

- ● Develop interpersonal communication skills

Grow on the Job

- Know how to learn

- Be able to read, write, and do math

- Listen and communicate well

- Be flexible

- Be willing to work as part of a team

- Provide outstanding customer service

- Have good self-management skills

- Be able to solve problems and think critically

PART III

Teaching Hints and Transparency Masters

for

Creating Your High School Resume

By Kathryn Kraemer Troutman
Author of *Creating Your High School Resume*

Overview

This part contains tips and transparency masters to use with *Creating Your High School Resume*. I'm so pleased that you're using *Creating Your High School Resume* to teach your students how to write their resumes. Your students have most likely never written resumes. They will be wondering what to write. They will think that resumes are just for adults–people with jobs. You can tell them that their resumes have to start somewhere, sometime. And the time is *now*!

Students will worry that they have nothing to write about: "But I haven't *done anything*." You can encourage them by stating that they do have accomplishments to write about now.

Some students will have many activities, honors, and jobs. Other students will see–from the exercise of writing a resume–that they don't have much to write. *That is okay!* They also will see that they need to *do something*.

This is your students' first resume–the one that will build and change as they attend college and gain work experience. Their first full-time job after training and college may be a better one because they wrote a resume and kept track of their academic and job experiences.

If students see how important the resume is–how it reflects their skills, activities, and interests–they will recognize the importance of being proactive with joining clubs, developing skills, getting interesting community service assignments, and finding jobs that will add weight to their resumes. Resumes may need to be updated every semester to add new activities, jobs, grades, and other information.

Writing a resume and keeping track of school and work activities are very good exercises. Resumes can help students be more successful in life, because these written words represent their accomplishments and abilities.

I would like you to make resume writing a challenging, exciting, and personal experience. If students are down because they don't have information to include, remind them that it's okay. Encourage them to work on their skills, find the gaps, and create a plan to change. There's plenty of time; they're just in high school.

Some of the following transparency masters have more than one topic per page. You can place a sheet of paper over half of the page until you are ready to move to the next subject. This will save you from changing overheads and save on transparency costs.

Overheads have been created for most chapters. The chapter and page numbers under each transparency master refer to those in *Creating Your High School Resume.*

Transparency 1: Table of Contents (pages iv–v)

You will see that the book has eight chapters. I recommend that the students read the chapters before you review the material in class. You can decide how many days and classes you want to use to cover this text.

Here is a chapter overview:

- Chapters 1 and 2 cover the resume basics, such as why you need a resume and the different types of resumes.

- Chapter 3 is one of the most important chapters in the book. It starts the resume-writing exercises.

- Chapter 4 discusses skills. Students need to start thinking about their skills in addition to their academic and employment accomplishments. In fact, students need to know that they have skills—soft skills and hard skills.

- Chapter 5 is all about formatting the resume: type fonts, type size, page lengths, and technical formatting details.

- Chapter 6 is an important chapter explaining cover letters, reference lists, and thank-you letters.

- Chapter 7 includes case studies based on actual resumes of students and profiles of their objectives.

- Chapter 8 discusses four important methods of looking for a job: cold calling, networking, using the Internet, and sending direct mail. The chapter also offers interview tips.

If you can find the time to cover all eight chapters, your students will have the basics for resume writing, cover letter writing, and job search. This information can take them through college and beyond.

Encourage your students to keep a copy of their first resume. They will be quite amused when they look back at it after college. They will also see how much they've grown, changed, and accomplished.

Transparency 2: What Is a Resume? (Chapter 1, page 2)

Most high school students do not know much about resumes. Students will be surprised to think that they can even write a resume because "I haven't done anything."

The high school resume description is important for the students in realizing that they have "done something" that can go on a resume. High school is a critical time for students to explore their interests and crystallize ideas for the future. The resume will help them become more aware of their natural abilities and inclinations. Special courses, grades (if the GPA is over 3.0), honors, activities, sports, and other activities can be listed in their first resume.

Transparency 3: Why Is a Resume So Important? (Chapter 1, pages 2–4)

A resume is important because students are writing down on paper what they have accomplished. If they have accomplished nothing, then they have nothing to write. If they have accomplished something great, then they will be thrilled to put it on paper.

The resume becomes a diary or a logbook of sorts to keep track of accomplishments. Students will see the beginning of a good list and be proud of their accomplishments. They will be buoyed to achieve more—and to write it in their resumes. The resume can help build self-esteem and confidence in your students.

Transparency 3—continued: What Can a Resume Help You Do? (Chapter 1, pages 5–17)

Most students don't think they need a resume. But they don't realize how pleased employers will be if the student hands them a resume. Employers will be very impressed with the student's organization and the time taken to list education and employment. Many employers *expect* resumes.

A student can't apply for an internship without a resume and certainly cannot go to a job fair without one. When a student is writing his or her college essay, the resume will be a great record of achievements and information for the essay statement.

Transparency 4: Recommended Resume Formats for High School Students (Chapter 2, pages 18–33)

There are many types of resumes for professional people, but I recommend two resume types for high school students:

- **Chronological format:** This resume lists the most outstanding accomplishments by the student. This resume can be one or two pages, depending on the number of accomplishments.

- **Targeted format:** The samples in the book will show how important it is to target the resume toward a specific position or internship. The continuing case study in the book is for Emily, who has diverse interests, such as environmental work and a Department of Interior internship. Her skill emphasis is different for each resume.

You may have a student in your class who has diverse interests, also:

- Retail sales or working in an office

- Carpentry or pizza driver

- Medical office assistant or telemarketer

The skills required for each of these positions is different. If your students want to be considered for specific positions, you will need to encourage them to highlight their best skills that will support particular jobs.

Transparency 5: Resume-Writing Exercises (Chapter 3, pages 35–39)

Contact information is the easiest place to start with a resume. Students can quickly write their names, addresses, and phone numbers. You can remind them that they need to make their name stand out with large type—14 or 16 point. Discuss the importance of presentation and how they can individualize their resume with this first easy section.

Education is next because it is so important for students. They are in school full time, and academics are their primary activity. Students with less than a 3.0 GPA can omit GPA information. Students who have not taken special courses can move on to activities and employment.

Special classes are not limited to advanced placement coursework. They can be languages, computer courses, or other classes that are not standard curriculum. Students' resumes can reflect their interests in particular subject areas.

Transparency 6: Resume-Writing Exercises (Chapter 3, pages 40–42)

Honors and awards can be for academic achievement, sports, theater, music, and community service. Some students are recognized for achievement in their churches, synagogues, and community programs.

Activities are common for most students, and they will see examples in the book about the various school involvements. This will show students the importance of school activities for future college applications and jobs.

Transparency 7: Resume-Writing Exercises (Chapter 3, pages 43–49)

Workshops and lessons are often part of students' lives. Some take music lessons; many are very involved in sports or other special interests. Students need to include these activities in their resumes.

Internship and tech prep program examples appear in an extensive section in the book. While researching the book, I found that students in career tech programs did not emphasize their internships or list their specialized courses. These training programs will result in jobs! The work experience, courses, and certifications must be presented professionally.

The samples listed on pages 43 through 49 are outstanding. The samples will give the students ideas about how to best present their training courses. The tech prep programs and internships are as important or more important than a paid job.

Transparency 8: Resume-Writing Exercises (Chapter 3, pages 50–54)

Volunteer and community service work are required by many high schools before graduation. If a student can get a community service assignment in a field of interest, that would be great for the resume. For instance, if a student is interested in animals, a volunteer position with a veterinarian would be great. If a student is interested in medicine, a community service position in a hospital would be very educational.

Recommend to your students that they select a community service assignment that will enhance their resumes, help them with college, and give them early knowledge of a career.

Work experience is important. It might be baby-sitting, yard work, paper delivery, pizza prep, lifeguarding, or office work. Students need to write about work experience very carefully. They need to write a short description of the job. The samples will give them ideas of what to write and help them recognize the importance of work experience on a resume. They may be inspired to get a job that will add to their skills and experience in a field that they really like.

Transparency 9: What Are Your Hard and Soft Skills? (Chapter 4, pages 59–63)

In addition to education, activities, and employment experience, students possess skills. Students and professionals forget this frequently. Employers want to hire someone with the skills they need. Chapter 4 talks about two kinds of skills:

- Hard skills are specific technical skills gained through training and lessons. Students might take music lessons, use (self-study) computers, or have interests in construction, electronics, or science.

- Soft skills are very important, too. Some students have good communications skills and are outgoing. Other students are introverted but are detail oriented and analytical. Some students are organized; others struggle with organization. If you have a classroom of 20–30 students, you will have a diverse group of soft skills.

If the students will read the classified ads, they will find language describing "soft skills." An employer may ask for "an energetic person who has excellent communications skills, enjoys hard work, and who is organized and efficient."

You can ask your students, "How many of you believe that you are an organized person?" Besides getting a big laugh, you may get some students who admit to being organized. Others will admit that they are not.

Another good question is "How many of you enjoy being around other people, in a work setting?" Some students like working with people. Some students prefer to work on their own–in research, writing, mathematics, computer technology, or scientific laboratory work.

So each student will have different soft skills. Some very sophisticated tests can determine personality types. The Myers-Briggs Type Inventory is the most famous. Students can take this test when they get to college to find out if they are introverted, extroverted, and so on. This is a wonderful test for getting to know their strengths.

Transparency 10: Include Your Hard and Soft Skills (Chapter 4, pages 63–66)

To make a resume easier for the human resources manager or hiring manager to read, it is helpful to list skills at the top of the resume. The manager does not have to hunt for them or interpret the resume information. The Skills Summary can be listed after the student's name and address.

The student can change the Skills Summary to match the skills in the advertisement. It can be a very creative and "targeted" resume section.

Transparency 11: Select a Resume Format (Chapter 5, pages 72–75)

A traditional resume uses bullets down the left margin to emphasize the information. This is a good format for a student with a great deal of information.

In the contemporary resume, headings are on the left with margins indented. This is a good format for someone who does not have as much information and wants to fill up the page. The graphic resume includes borders and red, cross-type bullets.

In the scannable resume, the format is almost nonexistent. Everything is flush left. There are no bullets. If a student wants to submit a resume by e-mail or wants a resume to go into a major employer's database, this format should be used. For example, Walt Disney World has a resume database for summer employees.

It's important that each student's resume be individually formatted. If students use a word-processing resume template, all resumes will look alike. This is not good! Every student needs a distinctive resume. Contact me at kathryn@resume-place.com for a variety of resumes you and your students can use.

Students can choose any font that is easy to read. The most frequently used fonts are Times Roman and Arial. The student should use one type font throughout the entire resume.

Transparency 12: Formatting Checklist (Chapter 5, pages 79–80)

As you look at this section with your students, emphasize guidelines such as the following:

- Employers appreciate an objective. It saves them time trying to understand the student's desired job.

- Exceptional students may need more than one page for a resume. Students should use common sense regarding the length of their resume. If the information will help them get into the college or obtain the scholarship/internship, then one and one-half pages are okay.

- Students should use 11-point type if possible. To keep the resume on one page, however, they can reduce the size of less important information to 10 points.

- Using good paper is important. Cheap photocopy paper is not impressive, and the quality of print is not good.

- Good photocopies or laser prints are mandatory in this technology age.

- Be honest. The hiring manager will ask questions that will catch students if they exaggerate.

- Ask another person to read the resume before it's mailed.

Transparency 13: Grammar Reminders (Chapter 5, pages 81–83)

If the student has trouble with grammar, verb tenses, or punctuation, a teacher or good English student should check the resume.

Remind students to spell check their resumes but also read the final version for content and consistency.

Transparency 14: Persuasive Cover Letters (Chapter 6, pages 86–94)

The cover letter can help sell the student to the employer. If the letter is sincere, enthusiastic, and expresses the student's interest in the position, it can make a big difference. If students are qualified for a position because of skills they possess or courses they have taken, the cover letter should say this.

The letter should also include some keywords from the classified ad. The letter will then "speak the language" of the employer.

Transparency 14—continued: Impressive Reference Lists (Chapter 6, pages 95–96)

Give students suggestions for developing references. A reference can be a neighbor, teacher, pastor, physician, family friend, or employer.

Transparency 14—continued: Effective Thank-You Letters (Chapter 6, pages 97–98)

Say thank you after an interview! This is a great way to remind employers of an interview and to show that the student really wants the job. Enthusiasm, interest, follow-up: The thank-you letter can help seal the job offer.

No Transparency—Resume Case Studies (Chapter 7)

You can have your students study the resume case studies and find one or two resumes that they really like. Each student in the case studies has varying interests, skills, and experience. It's hard to believe that high school students can have such good resumes. Contact me at kathryn@resume-place.com for template information.

Melody Kemmer: Sophomore Loves Music, Dogs, and Volunteering

Calvin Kline: Junior to Become Airframe Mechanic

Gloria Ramirez: Sophomore Faces Challenge of Career in Skin Care

Kylie Jennings: Junior Has Many Interests But Uncertain Objectives

Matthew Manowitz: Junior Enjoys Golf, Looks Forward to Business Degree

Torraj Enayati: Senior Composes Music, Looks Beyond High School

Jacques Revellier: GED Graduate Plans to Be Veterinarian

Laura Redden: Senior Seeks Government Clerical Position

David Pastorelli: Junior Athlete Plans Career as Radiologic Technician

Danielle Edgington: Senior Seeks Summer Job in Government Agency

Siphiwe Mikhize: Senior Sets Sights on Mechanical Engineering Degree

Kwan Tak-Hing: Senior Moves Toward Career in Business and Industry

Roberto Mendez: Senior Takes His Place in a Family of Tradesmen

Nathan Brown: Senior Enjoys Leadership and Computers

Transparency 15: Job Search Tips (Chapter 8, pages 136–147)

Getting leads from adults makes some students bashful. But asking questions about job opportunities, careers, and earnings can be very helpful. Students can't be shy.

Reading the classified ads will make students more familiar with duties, salaries, and whether they actually want a job. Students might think that *any job* is good. That's not true. They need to read and understand the ads before they apply.

Cold calling takes nerve. But if a student stops by a business and asks if any openings exist, the worst that can happen is the employer will say, "No, we don't have any openings right now." The student could then say, "Do you ever hire students?" The business may hire many students. The student can leave a resume in case a job opens up. If this company is a desirable place to work, this student should call regularly to inquire about a job.

Perseverance pays when you're looking for a job! Perseverance is not "pesty"; it is being determined. Employers like this trait.

For students who like the Internet, a wealth of information is available for research. Students can study companies, industries, and job listings. It's incredible! The Web sites listed in the book are excellent to check for jobs.

Transparency 16: Interview Tips (Chapter 8, pages 148–150)

One of the most important points to know about interviewing is to be professional and relaxed but also to *ask questions*! The student should find out some information about the employer before going to the interview. If it is a local company, that may not be necessary because friends may have worked there. If the company is a new place, a student should try to find out how big the company is, who its customers are, and how long it has been in business.

It is important to be 10 minutes early so that a student is not stressed, rushed, and flustered. If the student sincerely believes that he or she can do the job and can help the company by being in that position, a student should say so: "I believe that I could do a good job here" or "I would really like to work here. I could learn this job quickly." It's okay to be positive!

Best Wishes to Your Students

A good resume can make your students feel good about their accomplishments. They will want to add more good grades, activities, jobs, and internships. Encourage your students to

- Keep their resumes up to date.
- Keep adding accomplishments and skills to their resumes.
- Believe in themselves.

Creating Your High School Resume

Table of Contents

Creating Your High School Resume
Transparency 1: Table of Contents, pages iv–v

What Is a Resume?

Dictionary: Short account of one's career and qualifications prepared by an applicant for a position.

High school resume: Summary of your high school career, including

- High school courses
- Grades
- Academic honors
- Extracurricular activities
- Sports participation
- Work experience
- Volunteer experience
- Special skills

Creating Your High School Resume
Transparency 2: Chapter 1, page 2

© JIST Works

Why Is a Resume So Important?

- Track education and work experience
- Recognize skills, interests, and accomplishments
- Save time when filling out job applications
- Make informed college and career choices
- Feel good about yourself and what you have done

What Can a Resume Help You Do?

- Apply for jobs and internships
- Apply to colleges and tech training programs
- Apply for work-study or co-op programs
- Apply for volunteer and community service work
- Find mentors, get references, and network

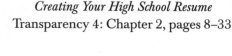

Recommended Resume Formats for High School Students

Chronological format: A complete compilation of your most important high school information. Good for college applications, scholarships, college fairs.

 Examples: pages 24, 31–32

Targeted format: Highlights skills for a specific job or internship.

 Examples: pages 23, 27–29

Resume-Writing Exercises

Contact Information

DARCY J. McHUGH

5343 West Mason Street

Palos Verdes, California 90089

(590) 888-0990

dmchugh@netspeed.net

Education

WASHINGTON HIGH SCHOOL, Lombard, IL

Graduation expected June XXXX

Overall GPA 3.0/4.0

Computer courses: PCs with Windows and Microsoft Word

Resume-Writing Exercises

Honors and Awards

- National Honor Society
- Varsity Basketball, MVP
- All-State Trumpet

Activities

- International Thespian Society
- Varsity Field Hockey Team, 2nd in league, XXXX
- Treasurer, Photography Club

Resume-Writing Exercises

Workshops and Lessons

- Writer's workshop, Loyola University, Chicago, IL, Summer XXXX
- Private guitar lessons, XXXX to present

Internships and Tech Prep Programs

Journalism

The Daily Breeze, Torrance, CA, Summer XXXX

Proofreader. Proofread typeset pages, including headlines, captions, and articles. Used standard proofreading symbols.

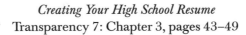

Resume-Writing Exercises

Volunteer and Community Service Work

Volunteer Office Assistant, Sierra Club, Chicago, IL, XXXX–XXXX

- Helped chapter officers coordinate activities and meetings.
- Assisted with member inquiries, mass mailings, and office operations.

Work Experience

Ski Liberty, Cumberland, MD. XX/XX–XX/XX

Cashier/Lift Operator. Experienced in handling very busy cashier operations. Skilled with maintaining ski lifts, ensuring safety, and using public relations skills to resolve problems.

What Are Your Hard and Soft Skills?

Hard Skills

- Electronics/engineering
- Construction/carpentry
- Graphic design
- Music
- Languages
- Computers

Soft Skills

- Flexibility
- Problem solving
- Decision making
- Patience
- Enthusiasm
- Creativity
- Hard working

Include Your Hard and Soft Skills

Skills Summary

- PC experience using Word 2000

- Proofreading skills

- Organized, efficient, and able to handle pressure

- Excellent communication skills

These targeted skills reflect the needs of the employer.

Select a Resume Format

Traditional: Uses serif type that is easy to read.

    Example: page 73

Contemporary: Uses sans serif type that is bold and dynamic.

    Example: page 74

Graphic: Uses lines, shadows, borders, and graphics.

    Example: page 75

Formatting Checklist

- No birth date or Social Security number

- Include an objective

- Try to keep to one page

- Leave out information about health in jobs that are not physical

- Use 11-point type and 1- to 1.25-inch margins

- Use good paper—white or off-white

- Make good copies—laser or clean photocopies

- Leave out negative comments

- Be honest

- Proofread carefully

Creating Your High School Resume
Transparency 12: Chapter 5, pages 79–80

Grammar Reminders

- Limit use of "I"

- Start phrases with a verb, if possible

- Be consistent with verbs and punctuation

- Make headings consistent

- Spell check and read for content

- Look for errors in contractions and possessive words

Creating Your High School Resume
Transparency 13: Chapter 5, pages 81–83

Persuasive Cover Letters

- Tell employers why you are qualified

- Use keywords from the job ad

Impressive Reference Lists

- Name of person

- Job title and company

- Person's work address and phone number

- Your relationship to this person

Effective Thank-You Letters

- Remind interviewers that you were in their office

- Show interest and enthusiasm

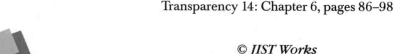

Job Search Tips

- Get leads from your network, mentors, parents

- Read the classified ads

- Cold calling

- Internet search

Creating Your High School Resume
Transparency 15: Chapter 8, pages 136–147

Interview Tips

Dress like other young people in the business:

- Clean

- Wrinkle free

- Not much jewelry

- Conservative hair

- Almost no perfume

- Conservative makeup

- Clean and reasonable shoes

- No backpacks, athletic bags, huge handbags

- Arrive 10 minutes early

- Breathe easy, smile, and look the interviewer in the eye

- Be confident—you can do the job

Creating Your High School Resume
Transparency 16: Chapter 8, pages 148–150

© JIST Works

Creating Your High School Portfolio,
Second Edition

An Interactive Guide for Documenting and
Planning Your Education, Career, and Life

By the Editors at JIST

Creating Your High School Portfolio, Second Edition, provides
specific, practical instructions for gathering, organizing,
displaying, and using portfolio materials. The workbook
shows students how to clarify their career and educational
goals, explore resources, and chart new directions. By
developing their portfolios, students gather information
about themselves that will help them make decisions
about future education, training, personal goals, and
career pursuits.

This clear, interesting workbook features dozens of
checklists and worksheets that students can complete
and place in their portfolios—along with career interest tests,
letters of reference, school information, resumes, and related documents.

ISBN 1-56370-906-6
Order Code J9066
Softcover • 160 pages
$8.95

- ◆ The workbook is designed to be used—not just read. The pages are perforated
  and three-hole punched so they can be placed in a portfolio or binder.

- ◆ Activities and worksheets take students step-by-step through the process of
  self-assessment and educational and career planning.

- ◆ The portfolio approach teaches students how to assemble a life history of
  experience and skills that can be easily updated.

Creating Your High School Portfolio, Second Edition

Table of Contents

Turn the page for information about *Creating Your High School Resume.*

Creating Your High School Resume,
Second Edition

A Step-by-Step Guide to Preparing an
Effective Resume for Jobs, College,
and Training Programs

By Kathryn Kraemer Troutman

ISBN 1-56370-902-3
Order Code J9023
Softcover • 160 pages

$8.95

Creating Your High School Resume, Second Edition, takes
students step-by-step through the resume-writing process.
Whether the students are planning to get additional
education and training after high school or are going
straight to work, this workbook helps them learn to
articulate and document their skills, interests, and
experiences into their first resume.

This book is not just for students with good grades,
lots of activities, and work experience. Many of the
resume excerpts and samples specifically target students who
do not have high grades, who are not involved in many activities,
and who do not have work experience.

◆ The workbook is designed to be used—not just read. Students should feel free to
write in the book and fill in the worksheets.

◆ Activities and worksheets concentrate on the various sections of a resume and take
students step-by-step through the process of creating their resumes.

◆ The portfolio approach teaches students how to summarize their experiences and
skills in a way that will catch and hold an interviewer's attention.

Creating Your High School Resume, Second Edition
Table of Contents